W0246939

ABOUT THE AUTHOR

Jon Tait is a distinguished educator and school leader from the UK with 25 years' experience in the education profession. He has held positions in schools and education trusts such as Director of Education, Director of School Improvement and Deputy Chief Executive Officer. His extensive experience spans strategic leadership in teaching and learning, professional development, behaviour management, raising achievement, and school improvement. Jon is also a renowned education author, and has published books on topics ranging from classroom pedagogy to educational research and school leadership. His contributions to the field of education have made him a sought-after keynote speaker for teachers, leaders, publishers, and parents at national and international conferences, sharing insights on all aspects of education and learning. His extensive knowledge of how children learn effectively, both in the classroom and at home, together with his own experiences as a parent, make him an expert in this field.

Produced for DK by
Tom Forge, Emma Forge

Author Jon Tait

Project Editor Sophie Adam
Managing Art Editor Sarah Corcoran
Managing Editor Katherine Neep
Publisher Sarah Forbes
Production Editor Andy Hilliard
Production Controller Isabell Schart

First published in Great Britain in 2025 by
Dorling Kindersley Limited
20 Vauxhall Bridge Road,
London SW1V 2SA

The authorised representative in the EEA is
Dorling Kindersley Verlag GmbH. Arnulfstr. 124,
80636 Munich, Germany

Copyright © 2025 Dorling Kindersley Limited
A Penguin Random House Company
10 9 8 7 6 5 4 3 2 1
001–350065–Aug/2025

All rights reserved.
No part of this publication may be reproduced, stored in or introduced
into a retrieval system, or transmitted, in any form, or by any means
(electronic, mechanical, photocopying, recording, or otherwise), without
the prior written permission of the copyright owner.
DK values and supports copyright. Thank you for respecting intellectual
property laws by not reproducing, scanning or distributing any part of this
publication by any means without permission. By purchasing an
authorised edition, you are supporting writers and artists and enabling
DK to continue to publish books that inform and inspire readers.
No part of this publication may be used or reproduced in any manner for
the purpose of training artificial intelligence technologies or systems.
In accordance with Article 4(3) of the DSM Directive 2019/790, DK
expressly reserves this work from the text and data mining exception.

The publisher would like to thank the following for
their kind permission to reproduce their photographs:
123RF.com: dolgachov 22, serezniy 28; **Adobe Stock**: Pixel-Shot 70;
Dreamstime.com: Alessandrozocc 40, Yuri Arcurs 26, Chernetskaya 83,
Fizkes 87, Dimitar Gorgev 89, Jenifoto406 68, Matimix 64, Melica 74,
Naruemon Mondee 54, Monkey Business Images 13, 15, Pbclub 62,
Pressureua 58tr (Icons), Psisaa 50, Syda Productions 10,
Brian T. Young 84; **Getty Images / iStock**: fcafotodigital 32,
SDI Productions 46, SeventyFour 79, svetikd 36, years 81

Other sources
Collins, Kevan. Foreword to *Working with Parents to Support Children's
Learning: Guidance Report*, Education Endowment Foundation, 2021.

A CIP catalogue record for this book
is available from the British Library.
ISBN: 978-0-2417-4430-7

Printed and bound in China

www.dk.com

MIX
Paper | Supporting
responsible forestry
FSC™ C018179

This book was made with Forest
Stewardship Council™ certified
paper – one small step in DK's
commitment to a sustainable future.
Learn more at **www.dk.com/uk/
information/sustainability**

A PARENT'S GUIDE TO

Effective Study Habits

Understanding how to support
your child to realise their potential

Jon Tait

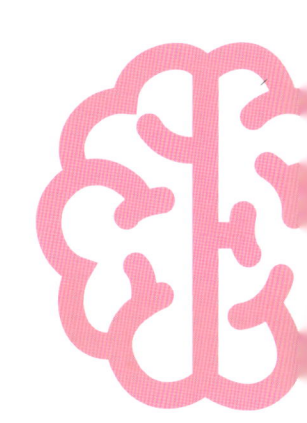

CONTENTS

HOW TO USE THIS BOOK

This book is intended to be an easy to "pick up and put down" guide that you can refer back to like a trusty recipe book in your kitchen. It has been written specifically so that you don't need to read it from cover to cover sequentially, but instead, dipping in and out of the different sections and tips as and when you need them.

1. THERE IS A ROLE FOR YOU

This section is all about why there is a role for you. It contains 7 short chapters that explain why parental involvement is so crucial. By taking time to really understand the importance of your role in your child's educational journey, you will then be ready to put the 25 study habits and tips in Section 2 into practice.

2. EFFECTIVE STUDY HABITS

This is where you'll find each of the 25 study habits and tips. Each habit is presented in a consistent format with helpful subsections explaining what it is, why it's important, how to do it, what equipment you require, what to avoid, and how to take it further. The habits are even more powerful when linked together with some of the other habits in the book, so you will also find a section that highlights which other habits to combine it with.

3. IMPLEMENTATION TIPS

This series of tips have all been written to give you helpful advice on how to put the habits into practice and make them work as effectively as possible. The advice in this section relates to all 25 of the study habits, making it a toolbox of knowledge and experience that will be the foundation for making the habits work.

ANATOMY OF A STUDY HABIT

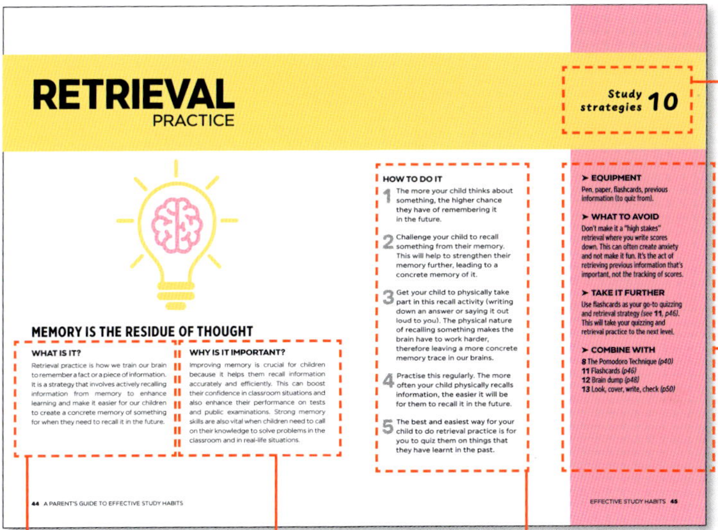

RETRIEVAL
PRACTICE

Study strategies **10**

MEMORY IS THE RESIDUE OF THOUGHT

WHAT IS IT?
Retrieval practice is how we train our brain to remember a fact or a piece of information. It is a strategy that involves actively recalling information from memory to enhance learning and make it easier for our children to create a concrete memory of something for when they need to recall it in the future.

WHY IS IT IMPORTANT?
Improving memory is crucial for children because it helps them recall information accurately and efficiently. This can boost their confidence in classroom situations and also enhance their performance on tests and public examinations. Strong memory skills are also vital when children need to call on their knowledge to solve problems in the classroom and in real-life situations.

HOW TO DO IT

1 The more your child thinks about something, the higher chance they have of remembering it in the future.

2 Challenge your child to recall something from their memory. This will help to strengthen their memory further, leading to a concrete memory of it.

3 Get your child to physically take part in this recall activity (writing down an answer or saying it out loud to you). The physical nature of recalling something makes the brain have to work harder, therefore leaving a more concrete memory trace in our brains.

4 Practise this regularly. The more often your child physically recalls information, the easier it will be for them to recall it in the future.

5 The best and easiest way for your child to do retrieval practice is for you to quiz them on things that they have learnt in the past.

➤ **EQUIPMENT**
Pen, paper, flashcards, previous information (to quiz from).

➤ **WHAT TO AVOID**
Don't make it a "high stakes" retrieval where you write scores down. This can often create anxiety and not make it fun. It's the act of retrieving previous information that's important, not the tracking of scores.

➤ **TAKE IT FURTHER**
Use flashcards as your go-to quizzing and retrieval strategy (see **11**, p46). This will take your quizzing and retrieval practice to the next level.

➤ **COMBINE WITH**
8 The Pomodoro Technique (p40)
11 Flashcards (p46)
12 Brain dump (p48)
13 Look, cover, write, check (p50)

44 A PARENT'S GUIDE TO EFFECTIVE STUDY HABITS

EFFECTIVE STUDY HABITS **45**

Easy reference
Each study habit is given a named section and number for easy reference. You can see suggestions for linking this to another study habit in the "Combine with" section.

Tips and information
The sidebar is packed with handy tips and information on what you will need and how best to implement each strategy.

What is it?
This section explains why it's important to adopt each study habit.

Why is it important?
The science, evidence, and reasoning behind why each study habit is important can be found here.

How to do it
Five step-by-step instructions describe how to put your study habit into action.

THERE IS A **ROLE** FOR YOU

GREAT **TEACHING**
IS NOT ENOUGH

Education has always been seen as the passport to our child's future, so a great deal of time is often taken in choosing the right school to send them to, with the hope that they will receive a quality education that will be the gateway to this future. We trust that teachers, with their expertise and dedication, will guide our children towards academic success. However, great teaching alone is not enough, and it is not the sole factor in a child's academic success. The idea that education is solely the responsibility of teachers is a common misconception. While teachers are indeed pivotal in shaping our children's academic lives, they cannot do it alone.

Even with a multitude of differentiated and bespoke strategies in our schools, children all get a very similar version of our lessons, but they all go home and end up achieving very differently to each other. Schools strive to provide equal learning opportunities for all children, with teachers delivering the same curriculum in classrooms designed to be fully inclusive. The reality is that children's home environments vary greatly, which influences their ability to absorb and apply what they've learnt within the classroom.

It's understandable that teachers and school leaders will focus most of their efforts on improving classroom instruction and implementing strategies to support children during school hours. However, while these efforts are essential, they must be complemented by initiatives that address the home study environment. Former Chief Executive of the Education Endowment Foundation, Kevan Collins, aptly noted, *"Despite our best efforts, the poorest students are still much less likely than their classmates to leave school with the qualifications they need. While much of this battle can be won inside the school gate, what happens at home is crucial too. We know that levels of parental engagement are consistently associated with children's academic outcomes"*.

→

Numerous studies have demonstrated that children who receive strong support, and where parents are actively involved in their education, perform better academically compared to their peers. Children with engaged parents also often develop better social skills and exhibit higher levels of self-esteem. Ultimately, a collaborative effort between home and school creates a nurturing environment that promotes a child's overall development. This support doesn't have to involve purchasing expensive resources or tutors. Simple, everyday actions can greatly enhance their confidence and motivation when facing challenges.

Crucially, we need to understand that a child's education is a continuous journey that extends beyond the classroom. A supportive home environment plays a crucial role in shaping a child's learning journey, irrespective of their age or stage. By working in tandem, teachers and parents can ensure that children have the best possible opportunities to succeed in their educational endeavours.

"A SUPPORTIVE HOME ENVIRONMENT PLAYS A CRUCIAL ROLE IN SHAPING A CHILD'S LEARNING JOURNEY."

WHY
PARENTS
NEED TO BE INVOLVED

Your active role in supervising and helping with study at home is invaluable. It not only enhances your child's academic performance but also contributes to their overall well-being and development. Here are some key reasons why parental involvement is so crucial:

1 Enhancing academic performance
When parents are engaged in their child's education, it often leads to better academic outcomes. Your interest and involvement shows your child that their education is important, which can increase their motivation and commitment to their studies. The more they are motivated, the better they will do.

2 Creating a structured and positive home environment
A home environment that values education creates a positive atmosphere for learning. Children thrive in environments where there is structure and routine.

This consistency not only reduces distractions but also signals to your child that their education is a priority. A structured home environment can help your child develop a strong work ethic and a positive attitude towards their studies.

3 Building confidence and reducing anxiety
Children often face stress and anxiety related to their studies, especially around examination time. Your presence and encouragement can provide a sense of security and help to boost their confidence and self-esteem. Knowing that they have your support can make challenging tasks seem more manageable and go a long way to ensuring that they do not feel overwhelmed.

4 Fostering a love for learning
When parents show interest in their child's education, it can inspire a lifelong love of learning. Your enthusiasm and curiosity can be contagious, encouraging your child to explore new subjects and develop a passion for knowledge. This positive attitude towards learning can have lasting benefits beyond the classroom.

5 Promoting personal development
Beyond academic success, your involvement helps in the overall development of your child. It teaches them important life skills such as discipline, time management, and perseverance. These skills are essential for their personal growth and future success, both in and out of school.

6 Strengthening parent-child relationships
Involvement in your child's education also strengthens your relationship with them. It provides opportunities for meaningful interactions and open communication. This bond can lead to a more trusting and supportive relationship, where your child feels comfortable sharing their successes and challenges with you.

By creating a supportive and structured environment, you set the stage for your child to thrive both in school and in life.

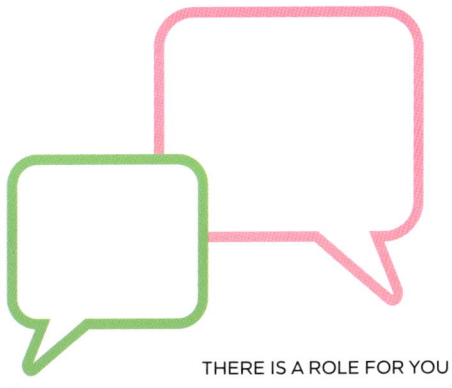

A DISTINCT LACK OF
TRAINING

While schools strive to provide the best possible learning environment within their walls, there is a scarcity of training, support, and resources when it comes to equipping parents with the tools and knowledge to support their children's education at home. This is not only about a lack of understanding for parents, but also a lack of training and understanding for teachers themselves about the importance of the home study environment and what they can do in partnership with parents to optimize this.

From the moment a child is born, parents influence their learning and development. However, as children grow and enter formal education, the focus often shifts entirely to what happens within school. Teachers, while experts in their subject areas and classroom management, may not always have the training or resources to guide parents on how to support their child's learning at home. The focus of teacher training programmes is predominantly focused on in-classroom strategies and curriculum delivery. As a result, teachers might not be fully equipped to advise parents on creating a conducive study environment at home. This oversight leaves parents feeling ill-equipped to support their children's academic journey, despite their best intentions.

The reality is that effective study habits are not just automatically developed through age; they must be taught and nurtured. Schools do an excellent job of introducing these habits, but without reinforcement at home, their impact can be limited. This is where your role as a parent at home is crucial. By creating a conducive study environment, setting routines, and encouraging good study practices, you can significantly enhance your child's ability to be academically successful. Yet unfortunately, many parents are unaware of how to do this effectively, simply because of a lack of simple and explicit guidance. This absence of training for parents means that many

are left to figure this out on their own, leading to missed opportunities for children to develop strong study habits that will serve them throughout their educational journey and beyond.

Schools may offer occasional workshops or parent-teacher meetings, but these are often insufficient to address the complexities of supporting your child's education at home. Time-pressed parents need clear, succinct, and practical guidance on how to set up an effective study environment and support a child's learning throughout their time in education. The practical habits and study strategies in Section 2 aim to bridge this gap by providing a comprehensive range of easy-to-understand guidance that you can implement immediately.

BAD HABITS
OVER GENERATIONS

As parents, we all want the best for our children and we strive to provide them with the tools they need to succeed in life. However, when it comes to studying, we often find ourselves falling back on the methods we were taught, or that were handed to us by our parents. With recent advancements in cognitive science, we have a wealth of knowledge about how we learn best, so it's important to recognize that some of these traditional methods may not always be the most effective. In fact, they could even hinder our children's academic progress.

Over generations, certain study habits have become deeply ingrained. We've probably all experienced the late-night cramming sessions before an exam, or re-reading our own study notes hoping that they will stick in our long-term memory. While these methods may have worked for some, research has shown that they are not the most efficient or effective ways to learn. Our children are growing up in a different era, with access to a wealth of information and resources that we could only dream of. This doesn't mean that we should discard everything we know about studying. Instead, we need to adapt and evolve these methods to suit the needs of our children.

It's our responsibility to guide our children towards effective study strategies and positive study habits. We need to be learners ourselves, continually seeking out the most effective ways to help our children study. This might mean unlearning some of our own ingrained study habits, together with acknowledging that the way we were taught to study isn't necessarily the best way for our children. It will involve trial and error, and it will definitely require patience. It might be a departure from how we studied ourselves, but it's a step towards equipping our children for success in this rapidly changing world.

Let's not pass on our outdated study habits to our children. Instead, let's equip them with the skills they need to become lifelong learners, and that starts with us, the parents, acknowledging that the study habits of the past may not be the best guide for the future. After all, the goal of education is not just to pass exams, but to ignite a passion for learning that lasts a lifetime.

"

THE GOAL OF EDUCATION
IS NOT JUST TO PASS
EXAMS, BUT TO IGNITE A
PASSION FOR LEARNING
THAT LASTS A LIFETIME."

THERE IS A SCIENCE BEHIND
HOW WE LEARN

Understanding how children learn is crucial for helping them succeed academically. We are now living in an age where we know a great deal about how we, as human beings, learn new information. We know the conditions in which we digest this information can make all the difference to how successful we will be in actually remembering this information in the future. Although you might hear your child say that they "like" or "prefer" to learn in a certain way, we now know that from a cognitive science point of view, there are more effective and efficient ways to learn information. This doesn't change based on what day of the week it is, or whether someone "likes" it or not, this is how our brains work. So while each child is unique, there are fundamental principles of learning that apply universally.

One of the reasons why this cognitive science research hasn't been more widely and commonly understood is that it has often been written in highly academic language by university professors and contained in long academic papers that are not accessible to everyone. One of the main aims of this book is to give you a simple overview of the most important information to know. This has been put into a series of habits and strategies that you can follow step by step with your child.

Within the book you'll be able to find habits and background knowledge taken from cognitive science on areas such as:

➤ **Silent focus** (page 34)
➤ **Desirable difficulty** (page 42)
➤ **Retrieval practice** (page 44)
➤ **Distributed practice** (page 52)

RETRIEVAL PRACTICE

It is worth looking at retrieval practice in more depth at this point as it is one of the most important principles to understand as parents when thinking about how our children can improve their memory of something. In simple terms, retrieval practice is a learning strategy that involves recalling information from memory.

This process of actively bringing information to the forefront of our mind strengthens the memory and makes it easier to retrieve that information in the future. Unlike traditional studying methods that often involve passively re-reading our old study notes or textbooks, retrieval practice requires an effortful recall, which has been shown to improve the long-term retention of this information.

When humans retrieve information, they are not just testing their memory; they are actually enhancing it. This process helps consolidate learning and transfer knowledge from short-term to long-term memory. Studies have demonstrated that school children who engage in regular retrieval practice (either independently on their own or with the help of you the parent) perform better on tests and retain information longer than those who do not.

A FAMILIAR EXAMPLE

To illustrate the power of retrieval practice, consider how many of us can still remember our first landline telephone number. This is probably not because we studied it repeatedly when we were young, but because we frequently had to retrieve it. Every time we answered the phone at home and recited our number to the caller at the other end, we were engaging in a low-stakes retrieval practice. Over time, this repeated recall cemented the number in our long-term memory, making it almost impossible to forget. The fact that you can now still remember this number (possibly 20 or 30 years after the last time you used it) demonstrates the power of regular retrieval practice.

The same examples can be drawn from old song lyrics. The reason that you can still remember these words is that your brain has had to regularly fetch this information and then you've had to actually do something with it, e.g. sing the lyrics. This physical action, combined with the brain having to work hard to retrieve the information for you to use, is the magic formula for an enhanced memory, especially if we want our children to remember something forever, not just for the day of the exam.

TREATING OUR CHILDREN
LIKE ATHLETES

Based on what we know about the science behind how we learn, we know that there are many different aspects that make us perform on any given task. It's not just about the effort that is put into the final exam. A good comparison is how this works in the world of professional sport. Imagine an athlete preparing for a major competition. They wouldn't just focus on their training sessions or the effort they put into the competition phase; they would pay meticulous attention to their overall health and well-being. They understand that peak performance is a result of a balanced approach to physical health, mental well-being, and consistent practice. Our children are no different. If we want them to excel academically, we need to pay close attention to their body and mind, as well as their studies.

REST AND SLEEP: THE FOUNDATION OF SUCCESS

Just as an athlete needs adequate rest to recover and perform, our children require sufficient sleep to function optimally. Sleep is crucial for memory consolidation, cognitive function, and emotional regulation. A well-rested child is more attentive in the classroom, retains information better, and is less prone to stress.

NUTRITION: FUELLING THE MIND AND BODY

An athlete wouldn't consume junk food and expect to perform at their best. Similarly, our children's diet plays a pivotal role in their academic success. A balanced diet is essential for brain development and energy. Encouraging healthy eating habits not only supports their physical health, but it also boosts their concentration and learning capabilities.

EXERCISE: BUILDING STRENGTH AND RESILIENCE

Physical activity is not just about keeping fit, it has significant positive effects on the brain. Regular exercise increases blood flow to the brain, enhancing cognitive function and reducing symptoms of anxiety and depression. For children, incorporating physical activity or even just a daily walk can improve their mood, energy levels, and overall academic performance.

CREATING A BALANCED ROUTINE

Balancing schoolwork, homework and academic study with rest, nutrition, and exercise requires a structured routine. Just as athletes have a training schedule, children benefit from a consistent daily routine that includes time for homework, physical activity, meals, and relaxation. This balance ensures they are not overwhelmed and can approach their studies with a clear and focused mind.

RAISING A
HIGH-PERFORMING
HUMAN

Developing good study habits and organizational skills is not just about academic success; it's about equipping your child with the tools they need to thrive in all areas of life. The skills and habits that lead to academic excellence are the same ones that will help your child become a high-performing individual, no matter what career path they choose.

ORGANIZATION AND PRIORITIZATION

Organization is the cornerstone of effective study habits. When your child learns to keep their study materials in order, they are also learning to manage their resources efficiently. This skill is invaluable in any career, where the ability to prioritize tasks

via calendars and manage workloads through to-do lists can make the difference between success and failure. This practice not only helps them stay on top of their schoolwork but also promotes and introduces a sense of discipline and order that will serve them well in adulthood.

PLANNING AND TIME MANAGEMENT

Planning is another critical skill that goes hand in hand with organization. Teaching your child to plan their study sessions and break down large projects into manageable tasks can significantly enhance their productivity. Effective time management ensures that they can balance their schoolwork with extracurricular activities and personal time. These planning skills are directly transferable to the workplace, where project management and the ability to meet deadlines are highly valued.

MEETING DEADLINES AND WORKING INDEPENDENTLY

The ability to meet deadlines is a crucial aspect of both academic and professional success. This habit of punctuality and reliability is essential in any career, especially when working as part of a team where others depend on your input. Additionally, developing the ability to work independently helps your child develop confidence in their own ability. This independence is a valuable trait that will help them navigate the challenges of adulthood with resilience and resourcefulness.

In the pages that follow, you will find helpful strategies that will help cement your child's future success. These skills are not just about getting good grades; they are about building a strong work ethic and developing a lifelong love of learning. The study habits and tips covered in this book can all stand alone and provide benefits, but the real magic happens when these strategies are combined, much like pieces of a jigsaw puzzle coming together to form a complete picture. By helping integrate all of the habits in this book into your child's study routine, you are giving them a toolkit of powerful and comprehensive skills that will set them up for life. With your help, they can become well rounded, high-performing individuals who are prepared to tackle the challenges that the real world will throw at them.

EFFECTIVE
STUDY
HABITS

DESIGNATED
STUDY SPACE

A PLACE WHERE YOUR CHILD GOES TO STUDY

WHAT IS IT?

Children need to be able to continue their studying at home and not just think that learning starts and ends in the classroom. It's therefore really important to think about where this can be at home, where your child can concentrate, write, read, and have the space to spread out their learning materials just like they would do on a desk at school.

WHY IS IT IMPORTANT?

It's important to find somewhere in the house where the conditions are going to be most effective for learning and studying. It's also important to try and ensure that this is a different place to somewhere that they normally relax in (e.g. a sofa or bed), where the sole purpose of the student going there is to study and not relax.

HOW TO DO IT

1 If your child studies on their bed or on the sofa, it is very difficult for their brain to get into a working mindset, because that place is normally associated with relaxing.

2 Your child needs to be able to spread their resources out and write on a flat surface such as a desk or a dining room table.

3 The study space needs to be somewhere quiet where your child will not be distracted. If this has to be the kitchen table, then they need to be able to use it when that room is quiet.

4 The room needs to be well lit from either a window, a ceiling light, or an extra table light. If your child has to squint due to poor light, it will give them headaches and result in mental fatigue.

5 Sitting upright in a chair to study, rather than slouching or lying down in bed is so much better, not only physically for the body, but also mentally to get them into a work mindset.

➤ EQUIPMENT
A quiet space in the house, preferably with a flat surface.

➤ WHAT TO AVOID
If the best or only suitable flat space in your house is in the kitchen, then try to avoid making dinner at the same time they are studying. You might feel your presence is supportive, but the constant noise will be an unwanted distraction.

➤ TAKE IT FURTHER
Think about putting a timetable together of when the space will be free of distractions, and when it will be "out of action" because of meal preparations. This way you and your child can know when they can use it and when they can be given a distraction-free environment.

➤ COMBINE WITH
2 Light the room *(p28)*
5 Silent focus *(p34)*

LIGHT
THE ROOM

STRAINING OUR EYES MAKES THINGS EVEN MORE DIFFICULT

WHAT IS IT?

Lots of bedrooms or designated study spaces are not well lit. This can be because the desk is in the wrong place in relation to the natural light from the window, or the room might not have sufficiently good lighting. All this does is make studying in these conditions much harder, thus reducing your child's overall efficiency and effectiveness.

WHY IS IT IMPORTANT?

If we want our children to be effective and efficient in their periods of study, then it is imperative that they study in the best conditions. Studying in a poorly lit room puts extra strain on your child's eyes, meaning they become mentally and physically fatigued much quicker. This leads to mental errors and wanting to stop studying much quicker.

HOW TO DO IT

1 Think about the layout of your child's bedroom or designated study space. If there is an option to move the desk, try to put the desk near a window so that natural light can light the study space.

2 In an ideal world, don't place the desk directly in front of the window (even though your natural inclination will tell you to do this). It can become very bright, meaning your child ends up shutting their curtains (therefore defeating the object of placing the desk in the light).

3 Putting a desk in front of a window can also create a big distraction to your child during their studies because they end up constantly looking out of the window (especially if the window is on the front of the house and there are passers-by and things to catch their attention).

4 Make sure that any supplementary lighting (ceiling light or additional desk lamp) provides sufficient light near the desk (and throughout the room, especially in the evening) so that it doesn't strain your child's eyes when reading or focusing on some text from a book or worksheet.

5 If the light is too bright or not bright enough from the main ceiling light, think about buying a different wattage of light bulb to change the brightness of the room.

Organization and environment **2**

➤ EQUIPMENT
A desk in a room with a window, bright bulb in the ceiling light, and desk lamp.

➤ WHAT TO AVOID
Not all light is great. If lamps and bulbs are too bright, they can cause just as much eye squinting as low light conditions.

➤ TAKE IT FURTHER
If space allows, position your desk so that the light comes in from behind the desk and your child is looking at a blank wall without distractions.

➤ COMBINE WITH
1 Designated study space *(p26)*

EQUIPMENT
READY

EVERYTHING WITHIN ARM'S REACH

WHAT IS IT?

One of the things that can cause interruption to your child's study flow is not having everything they need when they begin their period of study. It either causes wasted time to begin with when they should have already started, or it causes a break in focus and concentration if they have to get out of their seat to fetch something.

WHY IS IT IMPORTANT?

By helping and ensuring that they have absolutely everything they need before they begin a period of study, you are doing everything you can to create the perfect conditions to study in, without any unnecessary distractions that take your child's focus away from the task in hand.

HOW TO DO IT

1 Find out what equipment or resources your child needs before they sit down to complete a task or a period of study.

2 Depending on the task, they might require pens, paper, a ruler, coloured pens, revision guides, etc. This may also include a drink and maybe even a small snack.

3 Getting them a drink or even a small snack is also a good idea to keep them fuelled and also to stop them needing to get up if they feel thirsty or hungry.

4 Ensure that everything they need for that specific task or period of study is within arm's reach before they start.

5 Do a final check before you go by simply asking "Do you have absolutely everything you need?"

➤ EQUIPMENT
Pens, paper, revision guides, calculator, drink, snack, etc.

➤ WHAT TO AVOID
Don't be fooled by your child telling you they need their phone in the room because it's their calculator. They wouldn't be able to use this at school. Just get them a calculator.

➤ TAKE IT FURTHER
Keep study resources and stationary in a designated basket or box. It can then just be pulled out at the start of a study period, rather than trying to search the whole house for a pen or pad of paper.

➤ COMBINE WITH
1 Designated study space *(p26)*

DEVICE
DISTRACTIONS

WE NEED TO GIVE 100% FOCUS TO THE TASK AT HAND

WHAT IS IT?

Smartphones and devices have become the killer of focus and attention, especially when trying to concentrate or study. We have to get our children to learn to focus without distraction. Even if your child has their phone on silent, there is still the burning temptation to constantly check it for any notifications if it's within arm's reach.

WHY IS IT IMPORTANT?

If the phone is in the bedroom or at the designated study space when your child is supposed to be studying, then you can guarantee that their attention and focus will be constantly interrupted just because of the sheer presence of their phone. Therefore, switching it to silent, or turning off notifications is still not enough.

HOW TO DO IT

1 At the start of a study task or a Pomodoro period *(see* **8***, p40)*, inform your child that they need to give you their smartphone so that they can concentrate.

2 If your child tells you that it's on silent, this is still not enough. The smartphone needs to be removed from the room completely for the duration of study.

3 Tell your child that in their 5-minute break period at the completion of the 25-minute study period, they can get their smartphone back and check any notifications.

4 Time the 25-minute study period and allow your child to work in complete silence without any distractions or temptations within arm's reach.

5 If your child is slightly older and is worried that you will be looking through their phone, tell them they can turn it off, put it in another room or even remove the SIM card. All you want to do is just remove it from their reach, so they can fully concentrate.

➤ **EQUIPMENT**

No equipment required. This is about taking things away, not adding things.

➤ **WHAT TO AVOID**

If the first time you tell them about removing their phone is just before they start to study, it's going to cause a problem. This needs talking over and agreeing in advance.

➤ **TAKE IT FURTHER**

Check that the same type of notifications and distractions aren't also coming through on their laptop, iPad, Xbox, etc.

➤ **COMBINE WITH**

5 Silent focus *(p34)*
8 The Pomodoro Technique *(p40)*

SILENT
FOCUS

WE NEED TOTAL SILENCE FOR TOTAL CONCENTRATION

WHAT IS IT?

To give 100% focus to a task, and in order for your child to be able to think deeply about something, they need silence and no distractions. Even though they might say that it helps them, listening to music does not do anything to aid the learning process. In the vast majority of cases, there is no better environment to study in than complete silence.

WHY IS IT IMPORTANT?

In the exams your child sits, they will not be able to have their headphones on and listen to their favourite music. They will have to think in complete silence for the duration of the exam. Therefore, your child needs to practise in (and get used to) the same conditions in which they will be asked to perform in.

HOW TO DO IT

1 Ensure the designated study space (see **1**, *p26*) is somewhere quiet without any noise distractions.

2 Turn off any background music or televisions.

3 Do not interrupt your child while they are studying. Allow them that period of silence to think deeply and get into a study rhythm and sense of flow.

4 Remove any devices from the room that are likely to buzz, vibrate, or ring (see **4**, *p32*).

5 Communicate to the rest of the house that your child is starting a study period and that they need some quiet time.

➤ EQUIPMENT

No equipment required. This is about creating a quiet environment, so it might mean removing some things.

➤ WHAT TO AVOID

Do not use this as a punishment. Silence should be seen as something that your child wants in order to think and work at their best. It should not be seen as something that only happens when they are in trouble, or something you impose on them when they haven't been working well.

➤ TAKE IT FURTHER

Think about shutting doors and turning down the noise in other parts of the house when your child is studying (just like you would do if they were going to bed). The quieter the house is, the better they should study.

➤ COMBINE WITH

1 Designated study space *(p26)*
4 Device distractions *(p32)*

SETTING
CLEAR GOALS
AND OBJECTIVES

BEING ACTIVE IS NOT ALWAYS THE SAME AS BEING PRODUCTIVE

WHAT IS IT?

Children have a knack of going to their bedroom to study and then wasting so much time doing other things that they end up wasting a large proportion of the time in which you thought they were actually studying. We therefore need to help them develop clear objectives for each session and become more productive with their time.

WHY IS IT IMPORTANT?

Productive study time at home is crucial for children, especially when they have limited hours available. If children can learn to avoid distractions and allocate their limited study time wisely, then they can cover more material in less time, leading to increased chances of academic success.

HOW TO DO IT

1 Agree on clear goals and objectives for the study session. What are they going to do and why? Agree on a start time for the study session to begin and the duration of the study session (see step 5).

2 Ensure that the goals you have agreed on are achievable (within the time you have set and your child's prior knowledge and ability) and you have broken them down into manageable chunks.

3 Outline exactly what success should look like within that period of study so that your child can self-reflect on their progress and keep themselves on track. Without knowing what they are aiming for, they won't know how to achieve it.

4 Ensure that all equipment and everything they need is within arm's reach before they begin (see **3**, *p30*) and remove any distractions from the study space before they start (mobile phone, music, etc.).

5 Provide regular breaks and rewards by checking that they only work for 25 minutes at a time, followed by a 5-minute break (see **8**, *p40*). After their break, ask them whether they met their objectives and help them plan their next set of goals.

Organization and environment 6

➤ **EQUIPMENT**
Pens, paper, revision guides, calculator, drink, snack, etc.

➤ **WHAT TO AVOID**
If your child goes to their room to just "study", then there is a far higher chance of them not being productive as they spend time deciding what to do.

➤ **TAKE IT FURTHER**
Take some time to discuss with your child the times of the day when they feel they will be at their most productive. When are they most energetic and focused? This will vary from child to child, but it is worth thinking about when planning the times in which they will be studying (early morning, before or after dinner, etc.).

➤ **COMBINE WITH**
3 Equipment ready *(p30)*
7 Habit stacking *(p38)*
8 The Pomodoro Technique *(p40)*

HABIT
STACKING

THE BEST WAY TO FORM AND SUSTAIN A NEW STUDY HABIT

WHAT IS IT?

Habit stacking is a well-known productivity technique that involves linking a new habit to an existing one. By doing this, your child creates a mental link when an existing habit happens. This helps them remember to perform the new study habit consistently.

WHY IS IT IMPORTANT?

Getting into good study habits at home can be quite difficult to establish and even harder to maintain. However, if children can develop strong and automated study habits away from the classroom and it becomes part of their daily or weekly routines, then it won't need to feel like a constant battle between you and them to get them to study. The stronger the study habits, the more chance there will be of academic success.

HOW TO DO IT

1 Decide upon a new study habit that you would like your child to develop.

2 Identify a strong pre-existing habit in their daily routine that can be the cue or trigger for the new habit to happen.

3 Your child can attach this new habit either in front of, or after the pre-existing habit that you identified in step 2.

4 Practise the new habit with your child when the trigger or cue happens (e.g. after they brush their teeth, or before they go to bed).

5 Celebrate when you see the new habit in action. Positive reinforcement is essential for cultivating long-lasting habits.

➤ EQUIPMENT

This will all depend on what the new habit is.

➤ WHAT TO AVOID

Try to avoid setting new habits as a punishment or after a bad test or exam score. Habits should be seen as an essential and positive ingredient to being a productive student, not something that is only needed if you are not doing very well.

➤ TAKE IT FURTHER

If the pre-existing habit that you have chosen is something that your child enjoys, like watching their favourite TV programme, then encourage them to adopt the new study habit before this. That way, the pre-existing habit can also act as a reward.

➤ COMBINE WITH

6 Setting clear goals and objectives *(p36)*

THE **POMODORO** TECHNIQUE

THE OPTIMUM AMOUNT OF STUDY TIME

WHAT IS IT?

The Pomodoro Technique takes its name from the traditional tomato-shaped kitchen timer. In this instance, it means that each study period should only last for 25 minutes before your child has a 5-minute break. Each study period should be timed accurately to ensure your child is only studying for the optimum amount of time.

WHY IS IT IMPORTANT?

As humans we only have a limited amount of time that we can concentrate and focus for, without becoming tired or distracted. By continuing past that point we become mentally fatigued, begin to make mistakes, and we don't take in anywhere near as much information as before. It is therefore counterproductive to continue past that optimum time.

HOW TO DO IT

1 Ensure your child has everything they need for a set period of independent study or a specific task e.g. pens, paper, book/worksheet, snack, drink, etc.

2 Tell your child that they are going to work hard and focus 100% on the task at hand for just 25 minutes, at which point they will get a 5-minute break.

3 Turn off or remove any distractions from the room or their designated study space so they can focus and concentrate e.g. TV, music, mobile phone, etc.

4 Time the 25-minute study period and check that your child does not come away from the task and break their focus or concentration within that time.

5 Once the 25 minutes is up, reward your child with a 5-minute break where they can come away from their designated study space, stretch their legs, and you can then return anything you removed in step 3 so they can check on their notifications, etc.

➤ EQUIPMENT

A watch, clock, or something to time the 25-minute study period.

➤ WHAT TO AVOID

Avoid giving the timer to your child to time themselves. If they see that there's only a couple of minutes remaining, they might not think it's worth starting the next question, or moving onto the next task.

➤ TAKE IT FURTHER

You can easily schedule two Pomodoros per hour, meaning your child will get more opportunities to study more subjects and with greater focus and productivity.

➤ COMBINE WITH

4 Device distractions *(p32)*
5 Silent focus *(p34)*
6 Setting clear goals and objectives *(p36)*
14 Distributed practice *(p52)*
15 Study planner *(p54)*

DESIRABLE
DIFFICULTY

NOT TOO HARD,
BUT NOT TOO EASY

WHAT IS IT?

By getting your child to make learning harder for themselves, they are creating exactly the right conditions in which to remember something. By making something desirably difficult (not too easy, not too hard, but with just the right amount of difficulty) it forces their brain to work hard and think hard – both of which will help to strengthen their memory of it.

WHY IS IT IMPORTANT?

If studying is too easy because your child has just been learning it and it's still in their short-term memory, then they won't learn anything because their brain doesn't have to do much work at all. When they quiz themself on a topic that they haven't looked at for a while, this is when their brain has to work hard, thus creating a longer-lasting memory trace.

HOW TO DO IT

1 Identify either a task that you want to set for your child. Ideally this needs to be something that they have almost had time to forget (something that they were taught a few weeks ago).

2 Talk to your child about how easy or difficult the task might be. If the task is too easy, there will be a lack of motivation, due to a low level of challenge. If the task is too difficult, your child will quickly lose motivation because they will feel it is unachievable.

3 Find the sweet spot where something is challenging, but not beyond them. Talk this through with your child. The task needs them to work hard and think hard. It needs to be a challenge.

4 Monitor their motivation levels during the task to see if the difficulty level of the task has hit the sweet spot. You can normally observe this through body language.

5 Tweak the task or the conditions in which they are studying until you find the right level of challenge.

➤ EQUIPMENT

Task-based equipment (pen, paper, etc.).

➤ WHAT TO AVOID

Try to avoid just taking your child's word on what is too hard for them. They will probably tell you that something is too hard for them if it's quite a challenge. Take a look at their schoolbooks or age-related examination papers to see what they are expected to know and understand at their age/stage.

➤ TAKE IT FURTHER

Another way to apply a desirable level of difficulty and challenge is to get your child to complete the task under timed exam conditions. Create a time limit, remove any study aids, and get them to complete it in silence without any help or assistance.

➤ COMBINE WITH

16 Motivation and rewards *(p56)*

RETRIEVAL
PRACTICE

MEMORY IS THE RESIDUE OF THOUGHT

WHAT IS IT?

Retrieval practice is how we train our brain to remember a fact or a piece of information. It is a strategy that involves actively recalling information from memory to enhance learning and make it easier for our children to create a concrete memory of something for when they need to recall it in the future.

WHY IS IT IMPORTANT?

Improving memory is crucial for children because it helps them recall information accurately and efficiently. This can boost their confidence in classroom situations and also enhance their performance on tests and public examinations. Strong memory skills are also vital when children need to call on their knowledge to solve problems in the classroom and in real-life situations.

HOW TO DO IT

1 The more your child thinks about something, the higher chance they have of remembering it in the future.

2 Challenge your child to recall something from their memory. This will help to strengthen their memory further, leading to a concrete memory of it.

3 Get your child to physically take part in this recall activity (writing down an answer or saying it out loud to you). The physical nature of recalling something makes the brain have to work harder, therefore leaving a more concrete memory trace in our brains.

4 Practise this regularly. The more often your child physically recalls information, the easier it will be for them to recall it in the future.

5 The best and easiest way for your child to do retrieval practice is for you to quiz them on things that they have learnt in the past.

➤ EQUIPMENT
Pen, paper, flashcards, previous information (to quiz from).

➤ WHAT TO AVOID
Don't make it a "high stakes" retrieval where you write scores down. This can often create anxiety and not make it fun. It's the act of retrieving previous information that's important, not the tracking of scores.

➤ TAKE IT FURTHER
Use flashcards as your go-to quizzing and retrieval strategy *(see **11**, p46)*. This will take your quizzing and retrieval practice to the next level.

➤ COMBINE WITH
8 The Pomodoro Technique *(p40)*
11 Flashcards *(p46)*
12 Brain dump *(p48)*
13 Look, cover, write, check *(p50)*

FLASHCARDS

THE EASIEST AND MOST EFFECTIVE WAY TO RECALL INFORMATION

WHAT IS IT?

Creating and using flashcards is one of the best ways to get your child to learn and remember information. They are easy to create and can be used for any subject where there is key information to be learnt.

WHY IS IT IMPORTANT?

The best way to recall information and strengthen the memory is to use retrieval practice. Flashcards provide the perfect way to do this in a low-stakes way. It also enables your child to self-quiz themselves and get instant feedback, or for you to quiz them so you can take an active part in supporting them through their studies.

HOW TO DO IT

1 Identify the key knowledge that is required to be learnt from a certain topic (this might be from class notes, a revision guide, or a course specification).

2 Get a blank set of flashcards or cut up some paper to make your own.

3 Write a question on one side of the card and the corresponding answer on the reverse side.

4 Hole punch the cards in the top corner so you can tie them together (per subject, or per topic) via a keyring loop or treasury tag. This keeps them organized.

5 Take the cards off the loop and shuffle them. Ask a question. Get your child to answer it out loud before turning the card over to check for the answer.

➤ EQUIPMENT

A pack of index cards (blank flashcards) or just paper and scissors, a keyring loop, and a pen or pencil.

➤ WHAT TO AVOID

Only write one question on a card. It's nice to know if you answered that card correctly or not. If there are multiple questions, you will see all the answers when you turn the card over to check the answer to the first question.

➤ TAKE IT FURTHER

Take the cards off the loop. Every time your child gets a question correct, place it on a "confident" pile. Every time they get one wrong, place it on an "unconfident" pile. Then spend more time revisiting the unconfident pile with your child to plug key gaps in their knowledge.

➤ COMBINE WITH

8 The Pomodoro Technique *(p40)*
9 Desirable difficulty *(p42)*
10 Retrieval practice *(p44)*

BRAIN
DUMP

GET IT OUT OF YOUR HEAD AND ONTO A PIECE OF PAPER

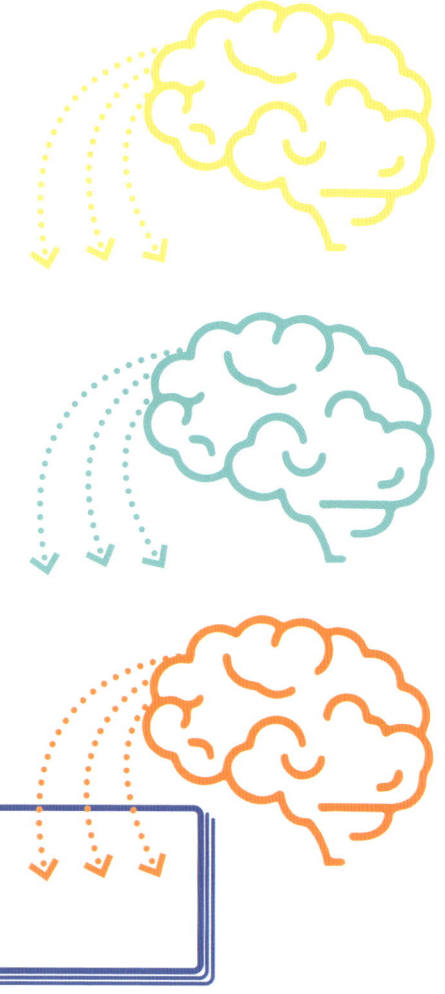

WHAT IS IT?

A great way for your child to do some retrieval practice on their own is to do a "brain dump" where they literally dump everything they know about a subject, out of their head and onto a piece of paper.

WHY IS IT IMPORTANT?

This is another quick and easy way to introduce retrieval practice and quizzing to your child. It requires virtually no resources or set up time and there are no difficult questions to potentially trip them up. How they structure their page is irrelevant. What is more important is simply having to retrieve information and then get it onto a piece of paper.

HOW TO DO IT

1 Decide on a specific topic that your child wants to recall and revise (not a whole subject, but a topic from within a certain subject).

2 Get your child to write down everything they know and can remember about that topic without looking at their notes. This can be in any format they like e.g. spider diagram, mind map, bullet points, etc.

3 Once finished, you can check it against their notes, knowledge organizer, or revision guide to see how much they have been able to remember (they can also do this themself if studying alone).

4 Get them to add anything they have missed in a different colour so they can identify (and visually see) the gaps in their knowledge.

5 Repeat this process regularly until they have fewer and fewer additions to their page, demonstrating that they have plugged their knowledge gaps and that they can recall all of the key information relating to that topic, time after time.

➤ EQUIPMENT

Pen or pencil and paper, plus a different coloured pen or pencil for additions.

➤ WHAT TO AVOID

Don't throw completed "brain dumps" away. It's good to keep them to see their progress over time. The more they remember, the fewer additions (in a different colour) there will be. It will fill your child with confidence to look back on previous attempts to see how much they have improved.

➤ TAKE IT FURTHER

To add some challenge, give your child a time limit in which to complete a "brain dump". This starts to replicate exam situations where they have to work under pressure to recall information.

➤ COMBINE WITH

8 The Pomodoro Technique *(p40)*
9 Desirable difficulty *(p42)*
10 Retrieval practice *(p44)*

LOOK, **COVER,**
WRITE, **CHECK**

CAN YOU REMEMBER WHAT YOU HAVE JUST READ?

WHAT IS IT?

Look, Cover, Write, Check is another very easy way for your child to visually check how much they can remember of something they have just read or watched. As humans we "presume" that if we have just read or watched something that we would be able to remember it, but it is very surprising how much we forget immediately after digesting it.

WHY IS IT IMPORTANT?

This is really important for our children to do because they need to know exactly what they have understood and what they can and can't remember. Just because they have read something or been taught something doesn't always mean that it will stick. Getting into the habit of self-checking for understanding and the ability to recall it is a great skill to have.

HOW TO DO IT

1 Get your child to read or digest some new information – this can be from a revision guide, a book, or even from a short video.

2 Now get your child to cover up that information so they can't see it.

3 Get your child to write down everything they can recall about what they have just read or watched (key information). This can be in any format they like, e.g. bullet points, spider diagram, etc.

4 Now get your child or yourself to check how much they have been able to actually recall and add any additions in a different colour.

5 Get your child to repeat this process regularly to check how much they can remember.

➤ **EQUIPMENT**

Pen or pencil and paper, plus a different coloured pen or pencil for additions.

➤ **WHAT TO AVOID**

Make sure that the information that they are trying to recall isn't too big. Start with just one page and ask your child to recall the key facts or key pieces of information. They should not be looking to write it word for word.

➤ **TAKE IT FURTHER**

Once they have demonstrated that they can recall key information, gradually increase the volume of information that they have to look at and digest before you turn it over and ask them to recall it. This might now be a few pages, a whole chapter, or an entire topic.

➤ **COMBINE WITH**

8 The Pomodoro Technique *(p40)*
9 Desirable difficulty *(p42)*
10 Retrieval practice *(p44)*
12 Brain dump *(p48)*

DISTRIBUTED
PRACTICE

SPACING STUDY SESSIONS OUT, NOT JUST LAST-MINUTE CRAMMING

WHAT IS IT?

Distributed practice is where study sessions are spread out over weeks and months in the build-up to an examination date rather than last-minute cramming the night before an important exam. This improves organization, prioritization, memory consolidation, and also reduces stress and anxiety due to the confidence of feeling well prepared.

WHY IS IT IMPORTANT?

The most effective and efficient way to memorize information is to space out blocks of study, leaving some time in between each one. This gives your child time to almost forget the information, so that when they quiz themself on what they thought they had previously learnt, their brain needs to work hard to retrieve this information, thus creating a stronger memory trace.

HOW TO DO IT

1 Sit down with your child and discuss why it's important to space out their study over a longer period of time.

2 Look at final examination dates and then work back from there to know when to start from.

3 Create a study planner to help keep you and your child organized and on track (see **15**, p54).

4 Space out study sessions so they are not all crammed together, leaving time to almost forget the information so their brain has to work hard every session.

5 Alternate between different subjects or topics when planning sessions. This variety can help maintain your child's interest instead of doing a number of sessions from the same subject back to back.

➤ EQUIPMENT
Study planner or calendar (see **15**, p54)

➤ WHAT TO AVOID
It might be tempting to plan lots of sessions together in one day (to get the study out of the way for the week), but regular breaks and time away from studying is just as important as the studying itself. Without the time to rest and recharge, your child will become fatigued, meaning they are not learning anywhere near as much as if they were fully rested.

➤ TAKE IT FURTHER
Help your child plan for regular and consistent study times throughout the week to help them develop a strong routine. Studying at similar times of the day or evening creates a familiar pattern that they can get used to and be prepared for.

➤ COMBINE WITH
10 Retrieval practice (p44)
15 Study planner (p54)

STUDY
PLANNER

ORGANIZATION IS THE KEY TO SUCCESS

WHAT IS IT?

A simple and visual way to plan when study sessions are going to be, helping your child form and maintain a strong study routine away from the classroom.

WHY IS IT IMPORTANT?

In the majority of cases, the more organized and disciplined students are, the better they perform at school than their peers. Developing familiar routines at home for when and where they will study throughout the week is an important factor in helping to make this happen.

HOW TO DO IT

1 Use a calendar or create your own using a printable calendar template that you can edit on your computer.

2 Working back from your child's exam dates, schedule and distribute study sessions throughout each week, ensuring that you have good coverage of all your child's subjects (see **14**, *p52*). Schedule more frequent sessions to either more difficult subjects, or ones with the earliest examination dates.

3 Colour-code different subjects to make it easy to see at a glance.

4 Add sports clubs, events, and hobbies so that everything in your child's life is organized on the planner and nothing gets missed or overlooked.

5 Print and display it somewhere in the house (possibly on the fridge) so that your child can be held accountable for it.

➤ EQUIPMENT

Calendar or printable calendar template that can be edited.

➤ WHAT TO AVOID

Ensure that this is a joint process with your child. If you just create this yourself and impose it on your child without involving them in the planning process it can result in a lack of ownership and motivation. The study planner needs to be something you have both agreed on. It's also important to avoid just filling it with academic related information. By adding clubs, activities and other interesting things in your child's life, it will be more meaningful and serve as a personal calendar, not just as a study planner.

➤ TAKE IT FURTHER

Plan for only two weeks at a time. This allows you to review how each week goes and make necessary adjustments in the weeks ahead. You might find you need to change the times of some sessions. A rigid schedule that doesn't allow for adjustments can be counterproductive.

➤ COMBINE WITH

14 Distributed practice *(p52)*

MOTIVATION
AND REWARDS

RECOGNISING AND REWARDING YOUR CHILD FOR THEIR HARD WORK

WHAT IS IT?

Learning and studying for an upcoming exam can be quite difficult for a lot of young people. It takes time, commitment, effort, and energy. As parents we need to be the ones at home that are supporting, motivating, and rewarding our children through this tough academic time.

WHY IS IT IMPORTANT?

Even if your child is academically motivated in the run up to the examination season, there is bound to come a time when the amount of exams and the length of time sat in exams begins to take its toll. Rather than have this come as a surprise to you, we should be aware of this from the beginning and plan our motivation and rewards strategy accordingly

HOW TO DO IT

1 Show interest in your child's studies by discussing their progress and offering assistance when needed. Be their study buddy if possible and engage in discussions to reinforce their understanding of the subject matter.

2 Be prepared to sit in the same room with your child when they study (if required) in order to show your support and motivate them to ensure the study session happens in the way that you want it to.

3 Help your child break down their study goals into smaller, achievable tasks. This approach not only makes the workload seem more manageable but also provides a sense of accomplishment after completing each task.

4 Encourage your child to take short breaks in between study sessions. Studying for long hours without breaks can lead to burnout and a lack of motivation.

5 Rewards need not always be grand gestures. Celebrate every small achievement your child makes during their exam preparation. Acknowledgement and encouragement go a long way in boosting motivation.

➤ EQUIPMENT

Small rewards, giving up some of your own time, personal touches, and motivational language to demonstrate that hard work is always beneficial for them in the long term.

➤ WHAT TO AVOID

Rewards don't always have to be grand gestures. Small personal touches are often the nicest and most appreciated. Avoid getting into a situation where your child will only study if there is a physical (and expensive) reward at the end of it. This type of extrinsic motivation can lead to a culture where they only agree to something if they think that there is something materialistic on offer to them.

➤ TAKE IT FURTHER

Look at the exam calendar and try to judge when there is going to be a particularly tough week for your child (this might be due to some difficult subjects, or just the sheer volume of exams in one day or week). Plan for a nice reward around this time to either motivate them to do well in this week, or reward them after the week has finished.

➤ COMBINE WITH

15 Study planner *(p54)*

POSITIVE STRESS

STRESS CAN BE GOOD!

WHAT IS IT?

At various points throughout the year, you may often see your child grappling with stress and anxiety. While it's natural for us as parents to want our children to be calm and relaxed, a lot of the natural signs of stress that we see are just the body's natural response to challenges, and when harnessed positively, it can boost performance and enhance your child's readiness for exams.

WHY IS IT IMPORTANT?

Stress can be a vicious circle. When your child feels stressed or sees the visible signs of being stressed (sweating, increased heart rate, or faster breathing), then this creates more stress. As parents we need to help our children understand that these are all signs that their bodies are adapting to the situation and helping them perform at their best. For example, increased sweating is a sign that your body is regulating its temperature, and deeper breathing is your body's way of getting more oxygen around the body to the places that need it most. We need to get them to think of it as a benefit, not something to worry about.

HOW TO DO IT

1 Take time to sit down with your child and discuss the science behind stress and what is really happening in their body at that time.

2 Tell your child that when they feel stressed, their heart rate increases, pumping more blood and oxygen to their brains and muscles. This heightened blood flow will enhance their cognitive functions, sharpen their focus, and improve their memory recall.

3 Tell your child that stress can trigger changes in their breathing patterns, such as faster and shallower breaths. While this might seem disconcerting, it actually helps them deliver more oxygen to their brain and muscles, improving their overall performance.

4 Tell your child that sweating is a natural bodily response to stress, designed to help regulate their body temperature during challenging situations. While excessive sweating may be uncomfortable, it indicates that their body is adapting to the pressure.

5 Tell your child that exam stress often creates a state of heightened awareness and vigilance. This will make them more alert to details and less likely to make careless mistakes.

➤ **EQUIPMENT**
No equipment required.

➤ **WHAT TO AVOID**
Avoid using the term "stress" in a negative way at home. All this will do is add anxiety to your child when they feel and see physical signs of stress themselves. Instead, try to reframe it as just the body getting ready to deal with the challenges ahead – and that has to be a good thing!

➤ **TAKE IT FURTHER**
Practise deep breathing exercises with your child that they can use when they start to feel stressed. This can be used either before an event to help them feel calm and composed, or after an event to try and bring them back down to a state of relaxation. Having a strategy that they are comfortable with will help bring them back down to a state of calm. They can use it whenever and wherever they are.

➤ **COMBINE WITH**
20 Movement and exercise *(p64)*

THE **NIGHT BEFORE**

WHAT SHOULD MY CHILD BE DOING ON THE NIGHT BEFORE AN EXAM?

WHAT IS IT?

If your child has been well prepared and has planned their distributed study correctly, then there should be no need to stay up late the night before an exam. This should now be a night when they can relax and get a good night's sleep, safe in the knowledge that they are mentally and physically ready for the challenges that the exam will throw at them the next day.

WHY IS IT IMPORTANT?

While it's natural for students to want to cram and work late into the night before an exam, all this does is lead to stress and tiredness, meaning they can't focus when it comes to the tough questions an hour into their exam. Therefore, it's actually counterproductive.

HOW TO DO IT

1 Make sure your child has everything organized and packed in their bag, ready for the morning. Doing it in the morning creates more stress and a much higher chance of forgetting something important.

2 Advise your child to stop studying early in the evening. If they've been following a study schedule via a study planner, then they should not need to be doing any last-minute cramming.

3 Get your child to relax and rest their mind by doing something that they find enjoyable and relaxing, like watching a favourite film. Last-minute cramming usually leads to late-night anxiety and lots of tossing and turning in bed.

4 Try to get them to avoid caffeine, heavy meals, and electronic devices close to bedtime to ensure a restful sleep.

5 Getting between 8 and 10 hours of sleep is important if they want to be able to concentrate and focus to the best of their ability the next morning.

➤ EQUIPMENT
A relaxing environment.

➤ WHAT TO AVOID
Try to avoid placing too much emphasis on the fact that it is "the night before the big exam". All this will do is heighten anxiety levels (for you and them) and create the opposite environment to the one that you want. Everything you do should be in pursuit of relaxation and reduced stress levels that evening.

➤ TAKE IT FURTHER
Think about planning something nice to do with them on that evening once they are organized for the next day. Maybe sitting down together as a family to watch something, or going out for a nice relaxing walk. This way you can control what happens, rather than leaving it to chance.

➤ COMBINE WITH
19 You can't fool your body the night before an exam *(p62)*
21 Rest and sleep *(p66)*

YOU CAN'T FOOL YOUR BODY
THE NIGHT BEFORE AN EXAM

THE LAST PLACE YOU WANT TO BE MAKING LAST-MINUTE CHANGES TO YOUR ROUTINE

WHAT IS IT?

One of the common problems that children run into around exam season is that they try to make significant changes to their body clock at the last minute. But our body thrives on routine, so all this does is create unnecessary extra stress. This is why bringing your child's bedtime forward needs to be done well in advance of an important exam.

WHY IS IT IMPORTANT?

If your child is used to going to sleep much later at night (or even in the early hours) then they will not be sufficiently tired if they suddenly try to get an early night's sleep the night before an exam. By not being sufficiently tired, they will undoubtedly have difficulty falling asleep. If they are not able to fall asleep quickly, this will become stressful and increase anxiety levels as they toss and turn in bed.

HOW TO DO IT

1 Sit down with your child and look at the upcoming examination dates. Discuss the importance of getting sufficient sleep before an exam *(see **21**, p66)* and the need to bring their bedtime forward.

2 Start moving bedtime earlier by 15 minutes each night a week before the exam. This gradual change helps the body adjust without causing too much disruption.

3 Establish a calming pre-sleep routine, such as getting them to read a book or take a bath. This consistency signals to the body that it's time to wind down.

4 Try to get your child to reduce their exposure to screens (phones, tablets, computers) at least an hour before bedtime (you may want to create a designated charging spot in the house for everyone to place their phones overnight). The blue light from screens can interfere with the production of melatonin, the sleep hormone.

5 Ensure the bedroom is cool, dark, and quiet. Consider using blackout curtains if light from outside the bedroom is making it difficult to get to sleep.

➤ EQUIPMENT
Blackout curtains if required.

➤ WHAT TO AVOID
Avoid letting your child tell you that they don't need much sleep and that they can survive on a reduced amount of hours. Irrespective of personality, the human body requires a certain amount of rest and sleep in order to function at its very best the next day. For 13-18 year olds this is 8-10 hours per night.

➤ TAKE IT FURTHER
During peak examination season, try to get your child to keep similar bedtimes even at weekends. This way their body won't have to keep re-adjusting on a Sunday evening, meaning that they can keep their body clock as stable as possible during this important time.

➤ COMBINE WITH
18 The night before *(p60)*
21 Rest and sleep *(p66)*

MOVEMENT
AND EXERCISE

ACTIVE BODIES AND ACTIVE MINDS

WHAT IS IT?

Although we often focus on the academic side of learning and preparing for exams, it's essential not to overlook the importance of physical exercise during this critical period. Engaging in regular physical activity can significantly enhance your child's learning process and their overall academic success.

WHY IS IT IMPORTANT?

When your child exercises, their brain begins releasing chemicals called neurotransmitters, such as dopamine and serotonin, which are responsible for mood regulation and enhanced focus. This boost in brain chemicals can lead to improved attention, memory, and problem-solving skills – all of which are crucial as part of the learning process, especially during exams.

HOW TO DO IT

1 Sit down with your child to discuss the importance of exercise during study, as well as setting achievable exercise goals, such as 20–30 minutes of physical activity per day. Breaking it down into manageable chunks will make it less daunting.

2 Encourage your child to physically get up out of their seat in between regular 25-minute Pomodoro sets of study time *(see **8**, p40)*. This allows the blood and oxygen to increase the rate at which it is being pumped around the body, meaning that it's the best way for your child to almost have a physical reset, before sitting down and starting again.

3 Encourage your child to get up and go to the toilet or make themself a drink in between study sessions rather than sitting for hours on end trying to study without getting up.

4 Encourage your child to engage in physical activities they enjoy, such as sports or even a simple daily walk.

5 Plan study sessions around the sports clubs and fixtures that they already have. Don't remove these events from their schedule. Exercise should be seen as another essential ingredient in the study planner *(see **15**, p54)*.

Peak performance 20

➤ **EQUIPMENT**
Outdoor spaces, fresh air, sports practices.

➤ **WHAT TO AVOID**
Avoid making this seem like a huge task, or like it is a new keep-fit regime, especially if your child is not already regularly active. The last thing your child will want is the extra stress of having to start something new during the most stressful academic time of their life. Simple, regular exercise in the fresh air is all that is required.

➤ **TAKE IT FURTHER**
Join your child in their exercise routine to ensure it happens and to help keep them on track. Make it something that you are going to do together where you need each other's support. This not only provides motivation but might also offer some quality bonding time.

➤ **COMBINE WITH**
8 The Pomodoro Technique *(p40)*
15 Study planner *(p54)*
17 Positive stress *(p58)*

REST AND SLEEP

THE ESSENTIAL EVERYDAY INGREDIENT TO EFFECTIVE LEARNING

WHAT IS IT?

Making sure that your child gets adequate rest and sleep every night is essential for not only a healthy lifestyle, but it also plays a major part in the learning process. Being tired and mentally fatigued means that they can't focus as well as they normally would, meaning that they are nowhere near as effective or efficient with their study time.

WHY IS IT IMPORTANT?

Without adequate rest and sleep the brain struggles to process information in the same way, meaning that our children lose the ability to access and recall previously stored and learnt information. Tiredness also limits their ability to accurately assess situations, solve problems, and plan their approaches accordingly.

Peak
performance **21**

HOW TO DO IT

1 Actively managing your child's rest and sleep is essential if you want them to perform to the best of their ability.

2 Agree on sensible bedtimes that ensure they have sufficient time to rest and sleep before they need to wake up for school (8–10 hours per night for 13–18 year olds).

3 Help your child stick to those bedtimes. Getting into a routine and sticking to it will help their body clock and make it much easier to go to sleep each night.

4 Make sure the bedroom is cool, dark, and free from noise and distractions at bed time.

5 Try to reduce things like caffeine and blue light from mobile devices in the hour before bedtime. Both of these are signals to your child's body to be awake, not asleep.

➤ EQUIPMENT

Blackout blinds and curtains are good for creating dark conditions in which to easily sleep in.

➤ WHAT TO AVOID

Avoid using this as a punishment once in a while. Your child should value rest as part of the learning process and not see an early night as something that they dislike.

➤ TAKE IT FURTHER

Count back from your child's wake time to find the most suitable range in which they should go to bed. Ensure that their wake time also has sufficient time in which to eat and get ready before they leave the house.

➤ COMBINE WITH

18 The night before *(p60)*
19 You can't fool your body the night before an exam *(p62)*

EFFECTIVE STUDY HABITS **67**

BREAKFAST

THE MOST IMPORTANT MEAL OF THE DAY

WHAT IS IT?

Breakfast is often described as the most important meal of the day and this is vitally important for our children as part of their learning process. However, many children leave the house in the morning either without breakfast, or without a breakfast that is going to give them the energy they need to perform.

WHY IS IT IMPORTANT?

During the night as we sleep, our body uses a lot of energy stores for growth and repair, so our breakfast is used to replenish our energy levels, helping with our focus, concentration, and alertness. Skipping breakfast is simply not an option if you want your child to be a high-performing student.

HOW TO DO IT

1 Plan and potentially prepare breakfast the night before to save time in the morning. Involve your child in this process with you so they have ownership and excitement about what they are going to be eating and why.

2 Encourage your child to wake up 10–15 minutes earlier to allow enough time for a relaxed breakfast.

3 Choose whole-grain options such as oatmeal, whole-grain cereals, or whole-wheat toast. These provide sustained energy and help maintain concentration throughout the day. Avoid high-sugar breakfast items like pastries or sugary cereals, which can lead to energy crashes mid-morning.

4 For particularly busy mornings, have healthy grab-and-go options like fruit, yoghurt, or cereal bars. This ensures your child still gets a nutritious start even if they've woken up late and they are in a hurry.

5 Eat breakfast with your child whenever possible. Demonstrating healthy eating habits can encourage them to follow suit and understand the importance of a good breakfast.

Peak performance **22**

➤ **EQUIPMENT**

Healthy breakfast foods that yield slow-release energy.

➤ **WHAT TO AVOID**

Try to avoid leaving their breakfast choices up to them, or not knowing if they have even had anything to eat. Managing what they eat for breakfast (and if they eat) is an extremely important factor in how they will perform that day.

➤ **TAKE IT FURTHER**

Rather than seeing breakfast as something that is not very exciting, get your child to research what their favourite sports stars have for breakfast that sets them up for an important day ahead. This might give them a much better insight into what different foods provide the body with and why it's so important to take this meal seriously.

➤ **COMBINE WITH**

23 Set meal times *(p70)*
24 Avoid energy drinks *(p72)*

SET **MEAL** TIMES

WE ARE ALL CREATURES OF HABIT

WHAT IS IT?

Sticking to set meal times throughout the day allows our children's bodies to get used to knowing when to expect its next top up of food and energy, enabling them to effectively regulate their feelings, concentration, and focus.

WHY IS IT IMPORTANT?

Routines create a sense of comfort and regularity. This means they are not wasting brain power thinking about when the next meal is arriving, but are instead working out the complexities of their learning. Along with regular rest and sleep, the best way to ensure that your child is ready to take on the challenges of exams is to keep their body following strong routines.

Peak **23**
performance

HOW TO DO IT

1 Schedule meals for the week ahead, considering everyone's various activities.

2 Establish regular meal times and try to stick to them as closely as possible.

3 Involve your child in planning meals for the week. This can make them more excited about meal times and ensure the schedule works for everyone.

4 Make meal times enjoyable by encouraging conversation and removing distractions like their phones.

5 Be prepared to be flexible with meal times where necessary. Being 10 or 15 minutes later than planned shouldn't lead to increased stress for everyone. It should be a time to sit down and relax together.

➤ EQUIPMENT

A meal planner or calendar to show what is for dinner and when it's going to be.

➤ WHAT TO AVOID

Try to avoid (where possible) significant changes to meal times. Eating at similar times each day helps their body become accustomed to a regular eating schedule and reduces the likelihood of overeating or skipping meals.

➤ TAKE IT FURTHER

Incorporate your meal planning with your child's study planner. This way you can combine both calendars, ensuring that your child isn't planning a study session at the same time as you are planning for everyone to eat. This also allows you to see when the kitchen is going to be free from distractions if this is their designated study space.

➤ COMBINE WITH

15 Study planner *(p54)*
22 Breakfast *(p68)*

AVOID **ENERGY** DRINKS

THE THING OUR CHILDREN CAN DO WITHOUT!

WHAT IS IT?

In recent times, there has been a tendency for children to reach for high-sugar energy drinks as an artificial way to boost their energy and concentration levels. This can often be even more prevalent when the stakes are high, for example during the examination season. Water may seem too simple to be that effective, but if drunk alongside a good intake of high-energy-yielding foods, it will always be a more effective source of hydration, helping them to concentrate and focus.

WHY IS IT IMPORTANT?

Although energy drinks might sound like a good idea to children as a huge influx of energy right before an exam or an important study session, all they do is cause your child to have an "energy crash" when the effects of the drink wear off and their body begins to normalize again. If this is in the middle of, or towards the end of their exam, then this is absolutely not what your child needs.

HOW TO DO IT

1 Explain to your child that energy drinks typically contain high levels of caffeine, which can lead to jitteriness, increased heart rate, and even anxiety. For young, developing bodies, such high doses of caffeine can be overwhelming and harmful.

2 Explain to your child that consuming energy drinks before exams can severely disrupt sleep patterns. Adequate rest is crucial for cognitive function and memory consolidation, so disturbed sleep may negatively impact performance during exams.

3 Explain to your child that energy drinks may provide a short-lived energy boost, but this is often followed by an energy crash. They may find themselves fatigued and unfocused during the exam, hindering their ability to perform at their best.

4 Explain to your child that while energy drinks might increase alertness temporarily, they can also lead to difficulty in sustaining attention and concentrating for extended periods. This can be particularly detrimental during long exams that require continuous focus.

5 Explain to your child that many energy drinks cause increased urination and potential dehydration. Dehydration can impair cognitive function and negatively impact memory retention.

Peak performance **24**

➤ EQUIPMENT
Water and a balanced diet.

➤ WHAT TO AVOID
Avoid role modelling the need for energy drinks yourself as an adult. If your child sees the person that they look up to the most needing an energy drink to get going, then it will be extremely difficult to tell them otherwise.

➤ TAKE IT FURTHER
Spend time looking at habits Peak Performance 22 and 25 so that they can create a high-energy-yielding breakfast, together with drinking plenty of water to stay hydrated. This should provide your child with all the energy they need, without the need for any artificial and unhealthy replacements.

➤ COMBINE WITH
22 Breakfast *(p68)*
25 Hydration *(p74)*

HYDRATION

THE ESSENTIAL ELEMENT FOR MAXIMUM CONCENTRATION

WHAT IS IT?

Our children need to be well hydrated if they want to be able to perform at the best of their abilities. This is crucial during their time at school or throughout the summer examination period when they need to concentrate, think and focus for long periods of time.

WHY IS IT IMPORTANT?

A study into the link between keeping hydrated and children's performance in school found that drinking just 300ml of water can boost your child's attention by up to 25%. Drinking plenty of water on a regular basis has also been proven to help children maintain a good state of mental health and well-being.

Peak performance **25**

HOW TO DO IT

1 Sit down with your child and discuss the importance of keeping hydrated and all the benefits this has for their concentration and focus, especially during long exams.

2 Establish a daily water intake goal with your child and track their progress using a water bottle with measurements or a hydration app.

3 Ensure that water is readily available for your child by placing water bottles in their study area. This convenience encourages regular sipping.

4 Add natural flavours like lemon, cucumber, or mint to the water to make it more appealing for your child. This can make drinking water more enjoyable and less monotonous.

5 Get your child to use alarms or reminders on their phone or watch to prompt regular water breaks. Consistent reminders can help them establish a habit of drinking more water.

➤ EQUIPMENT
Water, water bottle, natural flavours.

➤ WHAT TO AVOID
Avoid getting your child to suddenly take on significantly more water (for the first time) on the day of an exam. If their body is not used to this, it could possibly cause them to need to go to the toilet during the exam. This will disrupt their thinking, focus, and concentration – not to mention the added embarrassment if they have to go more than once.

➤ TAKE IT FURTHER
Just like in moving your child's bedtime earlier 15 minutes at a time over a 7-day period *(p62)* try to get your child to increase their water consumption every day in the weeks leading up to examination season. This way their body will have adjusted in time for the exams.

➤ COMBINE WITH
19 You can't fool your body the night before an exam *(p62)*
24 Avoid energy drinks *(p72)*

IMPLEMENTATION
TIPS

AN INTERCONNECTED
JIGSAW

Imagine each habit as a single piece of a jigsaw puzzle. On its own, it may be useful, but it doesn't reveal the full picture. When you start to connect these pieces, you begin to see how they complement and enhance each other, creating a more effective and supportive study environment. For example, setting up a dedicated study space is a great start, but when you combine it with a flat desk, and a well-lit room that is silent and free of distractions, the impact on your child's learning can be hugely significant.

One of the key benefits of using multiple habits together is that they address different aspects of the learning process. Some strategies are focused on the physical environment, such as minimising distractions and ensuring good lighting, while others target specific study strategies

like creating flashcards or only spending 25 minutes at a time studying. Each habit is accompanied by a section that highlights other habits that work well in conjunction with it. This makes it easy for you to see how different tips can be linked together to maximize their effectiveness. These interconnected habits reinforce each other, making it easier for your child to adopt and maintain good study habits.

However, the goal is not to overwhelm yourself or your child by trying to begin all 25 habits at once. Instead, start with a few key pieces of the jigsaw and gradually build the bigger picture. As you and your child become more comfortable with each habit, you'll naturally find ways to integrate additional tips, creating a seamless and supportive study environment.

→

IT'S HARD,
BUT DON'T GIVE UP TOO QUICKLY

Embarking on the journey to establish effective study habits for your child can indeed feel daunting, especially if this is uncharted territory for you. It's important to acknowledge that the initial stages might be challenging, but remember, every worthwhile endeavour starts with a bit of difficulty. The key is to persist and not give up too quickly.

Creating the perfect study environment and instilling effective study habits in your child is a process that requires patience, consistency, and a lot of encouragement. It's natural to encounter resistance or frustration, both from your child and yourself. However, these initial hurdles are not insurmountable. With time and perseverance, you will see progress.

Think of this process as planting a garden. At first, the soil may be tough, and the seeds may seem slow to sprout. But with regular watering, sunlight, and care, those seeds will eventually grow into a thriving garden. Similarly, your efforts to establish study habits will bear fruit if you remain consistent and nurturing.

One of the most important things to remember is that change doesn't happen overnight. It's easy to feel disheartened if you don't see immediate results. However, it's crucial to stay the course. Consistency is your best ally in this journey. Establish a routine that works for your family and stick to it. This might mean setting aside a specific time each day for homework and study, creating a

quiet and organized study space, or using tools and resources that make studying more engaging for your child. The more consistent you are, the more these habits will become second nature to your child. While the path to establishing effective study habits may be challenging, it is far from impossible. With patience, consistency, and a positive attitude, you can help your child develop the skills they need to succeed academically. Don't give up too quickly; the rewards of your perseverance will be well worth the effort.

THEY MIGHT
NOT LIKE IT!

In our role as parents, we often find ourselves in the challenging position of enforcing rules and habits that our children might not initially appreciate. However, it's crucial to remember that our primary goal is to create a study environment that is conducive to their academic success, even if it means implementing practices that aren't immediately popular.

One of the most common points of contention is the removal of digital devices from the designated study space. In today's digital age, children are deeply attached to their devices, using them for everything from socialising to entertainment. However, these devices can be a significant source of distraction. By removing digital devices from the study area, you help your child focus on their tasks without the constant temptation to check messages or browse social media. While your child might initially protest, explaining the importance of uninterrupted study time can help them understand the benefits.

Another habit that might not be well received is the requirement to study in silence. Many children are accustomed to background noise, whether it is music, television, or something else in the background. However, studying in a quiet environment is crucial for deep thinking and concentration, together with mimicking the conditions of an actual exam. Silence helps minimize distractions and allows your child to fully engage with their study material. It might take some time for them to adjust, but the improvement in their ability to focus and retain information will be worth the initial discomfort.

Limiting multitasking is also a habit that can be challenging to enforce. Many children believe they can effectively juggle multiple tasks at once, such as studying while watching TV or chatting with friends. However, research has shown that multitasking can significantly reduce the quality of their work and their ability to retain information. This is also where simple mistakes are made due to the constant switching of focus.

It's important to remember that just because your child doesn't like a particular habit initially, it doesn't mean it's not beneficial. As adults, we have the experience and knowledge to understand what works best for creating an optimal study environment. It's our responsibility to guide our children, even if it means making unpopular decisions. By standing firm and explaining the reasons behind these habits, we can help our children develop effective study practices that will serve them well throughout their academic journey and beyond.

TALK IT
THROUGH

One of the most crucial steps in helping your child develop effective study habits is to sit down and talk through the strategies with them. It's not enough to simply tell your child what to do; they need to understand the "why" behind each strategy. This approach not only fosters a sense of collaboration but also helps your child see the value in what they are being asked to do.

Children, especially teenagers, often resist being told what to do without a clear reason. They are at a stage where they are developing their own sense of autonomy and critical thinking. By explaining the educational benefits behind each habit, you are respecting their growing independence and helping them to see the bigger picture. When your child understands that these habits are designed to make their study time more efficient and effective, they are more likely to embrace them.

For instance, if one of the strategies is to create a dedicated study space, explain how this can help minimize distractions and improve focus. Share with them that having a specific area for studying can signal to their brain that it's time to work, which can enhance concentration and productivity. When they understand that this habit can help them get their work done faster and with better results, they are more likely to see the value in it.

Another example could be the habit of only spending 25 minutes at a time studying. Children sometimes want to feel that they have done everything they can in the build-up to exams, so they spend hours and hours at their desk without a break trying to cram and remember information. However, as they become mentally tired, they end up being distracted and very inefficient with their time, meaning they are actually wasting time. Helping your child to understand this and plan for 5-minute "reset" breaks every 25 minutes will really demonstrate that you're here to help, not just to set rules.

By talking through these strategies, you are not only educating your child on effective study habits but also building a foundation of trust and open communication. Your child will feel more supported and understood, knowing that you are invested in their success and willing to take the time to explain the reasoning behind your guidance.

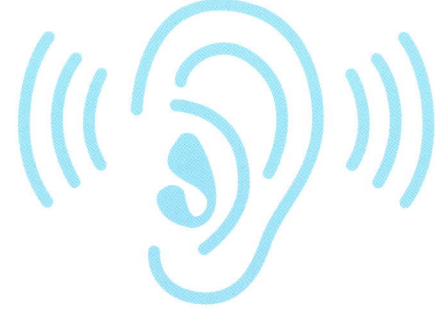

DON'T TRY TO INITIATE THE STRATEGIES
"IN THE MOMENT"

One of the most crucial aspects of helping your child develop effective study habits is ensuring that these strategies are communicated and agreed upon well in advance. Trying to implement new habits or rules on the spot can lead to resistance and misunderstandings. Establishing an effective study environment is challenging enough with teenagers without having to get into arguments every time they go to study. Clear communication can help avoid these conflicts and create a more harmonious home environment.

Imagine this scenario: you decide to take away your teenager's mobile phone while they are studying to minimize distractions. If this decision hasn't been previously discussed and agreed upon, it is likely to cause a significant conflict. Your child may feel blindsided and resentful, which can lead to arguments and a breakdown in communication. This is why it is essential to explain the reasons behind such decisions and the educational benefits they bring.

It is important to discuss why certain habits, like removing mobile phones and other devices during study time, can impact their ability to focus and be efficient with their study time. When you take the time to talk through these strategies with your child, you are cultivating a sense of collaboration and mutual respect. By doing this, you are not only helping them understand the "why" but also involving them in the decision making process. This collaborative approach makes it more likely that your child will buy into the new habits and adhere to them willingly.

Timing is everything though. Start these conversations at a time when both you and your child are relaxed and open to discussion. This could be at the beginning of the school year when you are talking about expectations at home, or at the start of the week when thinking about the week ahead in relation to when they will be studying. Use these moments to outline the strategies you believe will help them

succeed and invite their input. This dialogue is crucial for building a supportive and effective study environment.

Once you have begun to establish these agreements, it becomes much easier to provide gentle reminders when it is time to study. Instead of enforcing a rule out of the blue, you can remind your child of the collaborative agreements you have made. For example, you might say, "Remember, we agreed that keeping your phone away during study time helps you focus better." This approach reinforces the habit without causing friction, as your child is already aware of it and has already agreed to it.

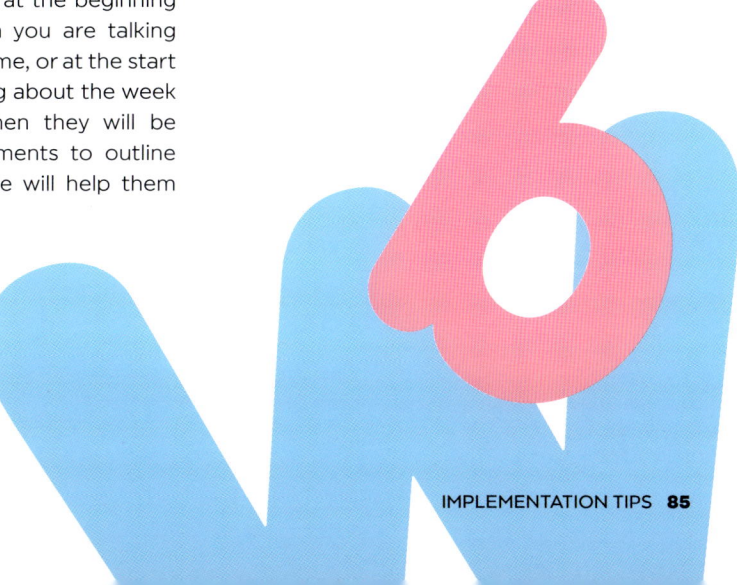

IT'S NOT A
PUNISHMENT

It's crucial for parents to understand that study habits and strategies should never be used as a form of punishment. If you try to use these methods to discipline your children when studying hasn't been going too well, it can lead to resistance and a lack of motivation. Associating negative connotations with positive study habits can have detrimental effects on your child's motivation and attitude towards learning, ultimately hindering your child's ability to learn and perform at their best.

Imagine a scenario where you check on your child in the designated study space and find that little progress has been made. They have been happily listening to some background music, but have not completed much work. In frustration, you now insist that they have to work in complete silence as a form of punishment. While the intention is to encourage focus, your child may begin to associate silence and concentration with negative feelings, rather than seeing it as a beneficial study habit.

Another example might be to demand that your child creates a study planner after you discover that they haven't been studying effectively over a period of time. While planning is an excellent strategy for managing time and tasks, if it's imposed as a punishment, your child may see it as a chore rather than a helpful tool. This negative perception can undermine the effectiveness of the planner and reduce their willingness to use it consistently.

The core issue with these examples is that they link positive study habits with punishment. When children perceive these strategies as punitive measures, they are less likely to adopt them willingly and more likely to resist them. This resistance can lead to a vicious cycle of poor study habits and academic performance, which is the opposite of what parents intend.

To develop a positive association with study habits, it's essential to present them as integral parts of a successful weekly routine. Try to emphasize that these habits are not just for times when they haven't been productive, but are practices that very successful people use every day to achieve their goals. By doing so, you can help your child understand that these habits are not actually punishments, but instead a set of valuable strategies that can significantly enhance their academic performance.

CELEBRATE
SUCCESS

It's important to recognize that creating an effective study environment at home can be challenging, but celebrating the successes along the way can make a significant difference. When your child starts to use study habits well as part of a consistent routine, it's crucial to acknowledge and praise this. Positive reinforcement will boost their confidence and encourage them to continue practising these habits until they become second nature.

One of the most powerful tools you have as a parent is your ability to notice when your child is doing really well, making a point of celebrating this. When you see your child sticking to their study schedule, completing assignments on time, or showing improvement in their scores and grades, take a moment to acknowledge their hard work. A simple "I'm proud of you" goes a long way in motivating them to keep up the good work.

It can also be really beneficial to acknowledge your child's efforts and achievements with specific compliments about exactly what you have been impressed with. Instead of a generic "Well done," try saying, "I noticed how focused you were during your study session today. Your hard work is really paying off!" This type of praise highlights the specific behaviour you want to encourage and shows them that you are paying attention to their efforts.

In addition to verbal praise, consider creating a reward system that aligns with your child's interests and preferences. Rewards don't have to be grand or expensive gestures, in fact the best ones are usually simple but meaningful. The key is to choose rewards that your child will appreciate and that reinforce the idea that their hard work leads to positive outcomes.

Consistency is key when it comes to praise and support. Make sure to acknowledge not just the big achievements but also the small, everyday efforts. Celebrate the fact that they sat down to study even when they didn't feel like it, or that they asked for help when they needed it. These small victories are just as important as the big ones and deserve recognition. By consistently acknowledging their efforts and achievements, you create a positive reinforcement loop that encourages them to keep going.

However, it's equally important to remember that not every day will go as planned. Teenagers are still developing their emotional maturity, and this, coupled with the many changes they are experiencing, can lead to complex mood swings. There will be days when your child might struggle to stick to their study habits or feel overwhelmed by their workload. During these times, it's essential to be patient and supportive. Remind them that it's okay to have setbacks and that what matters most is their effort and perseverance.

MY CHILD IS
NEURODIVERGENT;
WILL THIS WORK?

Neurodivergent children, such as those with ADHD or autism often thrive in environments that provide clarity, structure, and efficiency. The 25 tips provided in this book are designed to create such an environment, making them highly effective for neurodivergent children.

Clarity is essential for neurodivergent children as they often process information differently and may require more explicit instructions and clear expectations. The habits in this book are broken down step by step, so checking that your child is clear on each step is a good way of providing absolute clarity for them. By implementing clear and structured study habits, you can help your child understand what is expected of them and how to achieve it. This reduces anxiety and confusion, allowing your child to use their brain power to focus on the task at hand.

Neurodivergent children benefit greatly from having strong routines and a consistent daily schedule. This helps them feel secure and reduces the anxiety around adapting to new situations. Children with ADHD thrive when they have clear, consistent routines that help them manage their time and tasks more effectively. Similarly, children on the autism spectrum often find comfort and stability in the predictability of routines and

organized environments, which is exactly what the habits in this book provide.

As some neurodivergent children may have shorter attention spans or find it difficult to stay on task, the ability to be efficient with their time is crucial. Many of the habits and study strategies in this book are designed to maximize productivity in shorter bursts, making studying more effective. Techniques such as removing mobile phone distractions, only studying for 25 minutes at a time, and having everything available and within arm's reach before they start a study session can help to maintain their focus and engagement.

However, it is also important to recognize that every neurodivergent child is unique, and what works for one child may not work for another. Do not be afraid to make adaptations "in the moment" where necessary. There will be some days where no adaptations are required and other days when more patience and adaptability are needed. Understanding your child's specific needs and experiences is crucial. Tailoring these habits to fit your child's specific requirements may enhance their effectiveness and ensure a more supportive learning experience. It's therefore essential to observe and communicate with your child to find the right balance.

"NEURODIVERGENT CHILDREN BENEFIT GREATLY FROM HAVING STRONG ROUTINES AND A CONSISTENT DAILY SCHEDULE."

SUMMARY

When the "end of school bell" rings and our children head home, a crucial part of their education journey begins. This period, often overlooked by both schools and parents, plays a significant role in shaping their academic success, and is quite possibly the most underrated and underdeveloped area in our education systems. Parents play a pivotal role in creating a conducive study environment. Simple steps like setting a regular study schedule, minimising distractions, and providing necessary resources can make a substantial difference.

This book has been designed to bridge the gap between home and school, providing parents with the tools and knowledge they need to create an optimal learning environment at home. It is designed to be a comprehensive guide that outlines the significant impact that parents can have on their child's academic journey.

The 25 practical strategies provided are grounded in research and come with an easy to follow and consistent structure, ensuring that parents can implement them with ease. Each habit can be implemented on its own in isolation, or combined with another habit to make it more powerful. The structure and layout of the book has been specifically designed to enable you to pick it up and put it down whenever you're looking for inspiration, just like a good recipe book in the kitchen. You may want to read it cover to cover, but it is equally effective to dip in and out of as a valuable go-to resource that you will want to go back to at various points throughout the academic year.

Finally, remember ... this book has been written to help your child, not to punish them. Talk to your child about the study habits, explain the rationale behind them, use them to make them more efficient and effective in their academic endeavours and they will one day thank you for it.